The Clasp
and other poems

Wesleyan New Poets

Michael Collier

The Clasp
and other poems

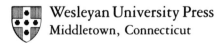
Wesleyan University Press
Middletown, Connecticut

Some of the poems in this book appeared originally in these magazines: *The Agni Review,* "The Angel of Memory," "The Clasp"; *The Antioch Review,* "Hamburg, St. Pauli District," "Bruges"; *Crazyhorse,* "Sand Figure," "Wedding Story"; *The Nation,* "In Khabarovsk"; *The New Republic,* "White Strawberries," "A Little Night Story," "Aquarium"; *Ploughshares,* "The Point of No Return"; *Poetry,* "Consider the Garden," "Flyer"; *The Seattle Review,* "What Heals"; *Shankpainter 22,* "Elegy"; *Sonora Review,* "Ornithophilous," "Night Waltz," "The Daughters of Degas," "White Bass," "Easter at San Xavier del Bac"; *Telescope,* "Ancestors," "The Bird Feeders"; *Three Rivers Poetry Journal,* "Baylands"; *TriQuarterly,* "Eyepiece," "The Lacquered Table."

I wish to thank the Fine Arts Work Center in Provincetown, the National Endowment for the Arts, and the Thomas J. Watson Foundation for fellowships that allowed me to complete many of these poems.
I am also particularly grateful to William Meredith, John Murphy, Steve Orlen, and Buzz Poverman for their friendship and encouragement.

LIBRARY OF CONGRESS CATALOGING IN PUBLICATION DATA

Collier, Michael, 1953–
The Clasp and other poems

(Wesleyan new poets)
    I. Title.   II. Series.
PS3553.O474645W5   1986   811'.54   85-8796
ISBN 0-8195-2128-0 (alk. paper)
ISBN 0-8195-1130-7 (pbk.: alk. paper)

All inquiries and permissions requests should be addressed to the Publisher, Wesleyan University Press, 110 Mt. Vernon Street, Middletown, Connecticut 06457.

Distributed by Harper & Row Publishers, Keystone Industrial Park, Scranton, Pennsylvania 18512.

Manufactured in the United States of America

First printing, 1986; second printing, 1987

WESLEYAN NEW POETS

For Katherine
and my parents

Contents

I

II

III

I

Ancestors

In the early days they called
their pliers *penguins,*
for like an arctic bird,
these were cold on the pain of abscess.
My ancestors stood over intricate holes
and did a jeweler's work
with an engineer's ambition
for immortality. Their large hands,
through the reduction of lenses,
became smaller and smaller,
until they fit inside of mouths.
These most intimate colliers,
with drill and bit and whir,
black slag of old amalgam,
the sear and singe of pulp.
They wanted to come as close
as they could to the fleshy rose
pulsing in the root like the heart's
faintest hint. Jewelers and brute
extractors, they filled the painful hollows
with alloys, covered withered
black stumps with porcelain
and called them *crowns* and *bridges*
and *jackets.* So they stood,
bully-shaped in their white coats,
knowing that the price of pain
is pain, father and son and cousin,
the whole practice among black machinery.

In Khabarovsk

Mud rising through thin snow,
and a dull welder's light
shining from the fires on the ice below—
as if from this quiet and vista
memory started out as a bright sun
against the completely unremembered.
Just as in another part of the city,
the thin Ussuri bends to confluence,
and Lenin Prospect ends at a granite
esplanade, steep gardens
leveling to a beach. In summer
families watch fireworks rising
from ghost-lit barges: this
in a travel brochure in my pocket,
which also shows the snow-covered square
in front of Hotel Europe,
from which I gauged the bend of my first walk
to this bank, without memory,
where beyond the fires
lay the blue horizon of China
and the barges setting out from there,
the lumberers with their last loads
of stolen larch, magpies circling;
and all the exhalations of horses and men,
like warm beats against the cold,
moved immunely over the snapping ice.
Then it was only in the river's name, Amur,
and after a long time
came a memory of love.

Hölderlin

Think of Hölderlin when you do not understand
how the execution of love is felt
in the strange revelation of absence,
and how on a post road in Provence, he bent
to examine the rigging a spider stretched
between two sunflower stalks, and as he crouched,
he saw the web's dark center contract,
leaving a silk target.

At a hostel he drank from a pewter cup—
turning red for the drops
that stained the Madame's shoes—
and finishing most of it, he found a spider, dead,
folded in the bottom of the cup; of course,
he knew his love was dead.

In the morning he decided that his life was someone else's:
a man who occupied a tower and wed platonic
Diotima. His thirteen daughters—
one of them a Pope, Sultan the next,
the third is Czar of Russia—still live.
Caught between desire and wisdom, he knew only
that his love had died, and he *Crazy, Crazy, Crazy.*

for Michael & Anne Hamburger

Elegy

Each morning of his Easter visits,
I opened the door to my room quietly
and found Grandfather sleeping.
His brown spotted head lay
like a gull's egg on the pillow.
Eyeglasses snug on his nose,

fogged with warm breath,
and his fingers curled over the blankets
like bean shoots.
Crossing to the closet, I sent
clothes hangers rocking, clanging
against each other, and wondered

if he'd wake to follow my blurred
form as I crept away.
When I was very young, he took me
to the race track,
and holding my hand
led me around the paddock. The horses,

covered with bright blankets,
stood separately in the large grassy
field; steam rising from their
dark heads into the clear air
frightened me, and even as he raised
me to place a lucky kiss

on his favorite sorrel, I thought
the horses were burning.
My lips touched oily thin fur
below the large eye that did not shut,
and turning away from the warm animal,
I lost Grandfather's eyes

behind his steamed lenses. This morning
the warm shadow
of that horse covered me as I imagined
Grandfather carefully clearing
the moisture from his lenses,
that special, circular rubbing

that allows me, all at once, to find
on the nightstand his blue beret,
Lucky Strikes, folded racing forms,
and in bed, sleeping,
favorite, tender horse.

The Angel of Memory

Each country you visited became a small
possession mingling with objects
in your yard—Russia caught in tangleweed,
Italy torn in the gravel path. One day,
you move the mower and find Greece:
a stone cottage, newly whitewashed,
an olive tree building shade around the outhouse,
two almond trees thin before spring,
and a plum tree you share with your neighbors,
who have stopped peeking over the wall
and come like friends into your yard with their dogs.
They bring pomegranates for your rabbits,
cracking the dried husks with blunt fingers.

A cloud blocks the sun for a moment,
and night fills the Greek village.
You watch Dmetri climb the fig tree
in Andreas's yard and grab a hen roosting,
then pop its head off before it squawks.
He runs through town with the hen trailing blood
and leaves the head at the kiosk.

In the white grass beneath the moon, you see yourself
running through the moon-calmed village.
You are looking for the Israeli girl
who wanted to live with you.
Soon you are near the old harbor
where boats rust to the color of pomegranates
and kelp tangles with chains and bowlines
like grass in the mower's axle.

She is as you imagined, watching an old man
raise a mallet to soften octopus on the dock.
The man is careful not to hit the ink sacs
near the head. The girl is so far away,
so small that her eyes, like octopus eyes,
are black with light, and her dark brows
arch like birds over the hills behind her.

White Strawberries

In the photograph she is not always
standing at the edge of the mowed field
clutching a bouquet of weeds for the mulch,

her ripped Wellingtons glistening from damp
grass and striped socks showing beneath
rolled-up pants. No, sometimes she floats

in the hazy marsh gas that rises in the reeds
behind her and the sun fills her hair with flames
that catch in the distant mulberry.

I've seen her disappear when wasps hover for
the dark berries and the air is clear,
the light endless; or she points to the fish-

monger crossing the garden, sole in each hand,
his palms bleeding from fine cuts and a pink
blush spreads at the edge of the wet fillets.

Perhaps all memory of that country enters
this photograph, like cows escaped from pasture,
because for her, I have no remorse; it was clear

between us. Like the white strawberries
she brought from the garden one day, small,
covered with a bristly down, and which I thought

unripe, but they were precious,
nothing but albinos in her hand.

Hamburg, St. Pauli District

How long did my black glove lie near
the streetcar tracks like a black
intention of my hand in snow—
a day, ten years?
I don't believe that what we lose
is lost forever. See, my memory
of you has survived like a poor
sentiment made trashy by a last desire
to kiss, though the room is full
of strangers and your husband
rocks your child gently
near the Christmas tree. Sometimes
we have nothing but the wrong words
for desire. Sometimes we just leave
these rooms and enter a stairwell
that has turned blue with the early
light of morning, and the earthly snow
outside is blue too. Sometimes
we reach for the gloves that are now
separated forever, and our white hands
that will make everything indelible
wave to the lovely women of St. Pauli,
who are thin and blonde across the street
in their leather pants, and the women
laugh at our gestures. Our hands
that cannot fall free of their wrists,
like gloves, to escape our next intentions.

Bruges

I dreamt of a Flemish city
that quit all commerce, drained its canals
and filled the empty channels with tulips
and mushrooms, and I dreamt of Betadine,
the orange paint of a surgeon:

snow fell from the sky
and a woman dressed in a green rain slicker
disappeared in the grainy world across the canal.
Soon I was touching the lathered sides
of a shaggy draft horse
at the back of a blind alley.
Ice nettled the horse's belly
and a stench rose in the mist of melting snow.
I wanted to make my way past death,
to use the horse and its black harness
and stop the snow falling
or stop the woman in her last shimmering.

Near morning the dream returned: the horse, fetlock deep
in snow, too large to turn around in the alley,
a feed bag muzzling its mouth,
and its stench, the stench of death,
frightened me, for I was aware
that the woman in the green rain slicker
had entered the room, and without looking
I knew she was just a few days beyond her death,

coming to tell me that there is no way past,
fresh from surgery in a green gown,
her head painted orange,
while behind her in the hall
snow kept falling.

The Point of No Return

Out of the dust and tall border grass
of an airfield appears my father, not
magically, but in a photograph.
A generation of fathers uniformed and standing,
married, absent from the birth of their sons,
who will be weak soldiers and fight the war
of an evil councillor.

My father tells me about something
he calls the point of no return.
That's when the plane he takes
from Natal, Brazil, to Florida develops
engine trouble and is forced to land
in a leper colony. He says that if you go
farther than halfway to anywhere
and you get in trouble, it's better to go
where you're headed than turn back.

The point of no return has to do only with
failures and the need to dramatize them.
Otherwise, the heart registers nothing.
Another story is told to explain success:
how the submarine his best friend captained
was torpedoed and sunk three days after
armistice. He sees his friend's face
in the occasional Japanese discovered
hiding in the Philippines.

Under the shade of palm trees the airplane
rests. My father stands under its wings
and puts his arms up in measurement.
He is young. His wife in Florida, young.
He has gone farther than halfway: the distance
forms a face in the dust of the cockpit.

Seneca Street

No more the black walnut's delineated
shade and the topped blue spruce
struggling in its overreach. No more
the double-trunked linden, the half-dead
mulberry, the thin maple and gnarled
sickle pear. No more the black cherry
and the weak apple, and, especially, no more
the dogwoods barely visible, fleshed out
now with leaves. And then, no more the two
floors, one of bright oak, the other
of random-width pine—trees all the same.
No more the black, mail-order door locks
that sag on the sagging doors with their
primitive crosses, and no more the anchor
stars that cleave to the brick like barnacles
and their long bolts threading the width
of the house. No more of this precise
nameable world. We will give it up.
We will move to a place vaguely familiar,
larger by rooms, closer to our needs,
which will emerge now as names for a new world.

for Bird

II

Two Girls in a Chair

Of the childhood photographs my wife
has given me, my favorite has her sitting
in a black alumni chair;
a college's gold seal and part of a Latin motto
curve beneath her right ear.
She's eight or nine, hair bobbed, dressed
in a white T-shirt and black tights
that reach only mid-calf.

She holds a neighbor friend in her lap,
someone whose leotards are ripped at the knees.
My wife's arms wrap around her friend's waist,
and her friend's feet dangle over the lily-
and fern-patterned linoleum.

Often when I enter my room, I notice only
this photograph, wedged among others,
and have felt a surprise of recognition
in those childhood friends
who could not now remember each other's name,
cannot recall what day of a New England summer
ended or began their long affection.

Baylands

The marsh is giving up birds to the clear lenses
of bird watchers in the duck blinds,
or the evening is asking that the silhouettes
of the loveless be filled with graceful shapes,
or those driving home look from their cars
and see the animal string move in the air
and wonder what it is that brings desire
so effortlessly to view.

I'm with two nieces, listening to their fears
about the narrow boardwalk leading to the bay.
The long planks supported by trestles
stretch over grass and damp earth.
This evening there's the possibility of sharks,
and I can't be trusted because I'm not married,
live in their spare room, and rarely shave.
Even the moon over Mount Hamilton is suspicious
as I try to find a face in something every child
knows is cold and dead.

At the tidal creek, where the sharks live,
I want to dangle them over the rail,
but it's too much like tempting bad luck,
so I make shark sounds and stomp the planks
as they huddle and giggle.

The opposite shore appears clear and crisp
like a miniature landscape, and as gull,
mallard, heron, some rare bird of instinct
rise from the baylands, I take my nieces' hands,
and watching grass give over completely to water,
we seem to rise as in levitation,
a human string connected by desire,
the common kind, as in being one with your blood.

Ornithophilous

Some come into the yard emotional,
sending up music as light as the muscles
that allow them flight, or they are quiet
and crimp the edge of the stone bath
where leaves float like small feathers.

Some come from the woods, the song predators
who find grain sacks in the shed or suck
clean the stamens from flowers in the window box.
In the evening, they stretch over the roof line singing
love is disease, love is disease.

I killed a kingbird devouring honeybees,
then broke it open with a rake.
The insects fell out stunned, but they dried
and rose like sputtering atoms. Some were dead,
their stingers lost in the bird's throat.

The carcass in the yard cracked like a doll's head,
yarn and sawdust spilling out, and the bees
spiraling off to their comb. Your hair covers
the pillow, your lips part while light escapes
from the lampshade, softening the darkness above the bed,

where I leave you sleeping each morning. The lampshade
with its painted cardinals, finches and jays
which you wake to as I stand on the porch
at dawn and listen to things that enter the yard.
Some that must be watched and some that must be stopped.

The Lacquered Table

All morning I've sanded gently
the blistered surface of this old table
your father brought from Brazil
and left outside for years.

I rub a wax-clogged tack rag over the powdery
varnish and the scene that must've
brought this ratty table so far rises.
I see you above in the window and point

to what's emerged. Dust flies from the rag
when I shake it, and how can I tell you
what this table says to me? That lovers
who won't stop forgiving each other

spread a black undercoat of patience
over a large area, then draw
red borders of specific wooing,
of long sleepless acquaintance,

and then the daily parrots and fruits,
equatorial flowers and vines that perch
and root over the black field.

Without looking, I know you are gone.
Fresh varnish bubbles clear and seeps,
darkening the lush painted garden.
Perhaps we have wakened from our forgiving

selves and see only water stains,
buckling veneer. Nothing that would stop
us from separating, not even maintenance
that love abides.

Sand Figure

If under bright October sun you lay
on the beach while a woman traced
your shape in the erasable sand,
and smiling at the pleasure of her hand,
you rose from your form,
when you returned from the water
you might find the woman had buried a stick
between the outline of your legs
and smoothed over a mound there
like a codpiece. You might be holding
a wooden sword in one hand
and in the other a plastic bottle
as a shield, crab husks
for laurel around your head. You might
see your mortal self in the brown
and black turban shells imbedded as eyes.

You might laugh at what you've become,
or lying next to your Achilles of debris,
you might ask the woman to choose
a lover. Though you're naked,
your feet stained with tar, salt
crystallized on your shoulders, legs
fuzzy with kelp, you'd have to convince
the woman that it is her you love,
and not what she's created
and not yourself.

Consider the Garden

I worry for the broccoli's sake
that it works too hard in this bad weather,
is too anxious to please me, or that it has seen
the eggplant and cucumber expand easily
in lascivious shade and has watched, as I have,
how those vegetables love only themselves,
hoarding their seed until it falls free
of their dark skin.

I want the broccoli to learn the ethic of busywork,
the ramshackle shantytown of green beans,
where piecework is sweet and profitable,
and the tiny delicate blue-and-white flowers
with lavender pistils are like the soft faces
of infants about to be baptized.

Such is my vanity when I look at the garden
that I think I can influence the destiny of plants,
can instruct them, or tell them, with my tending,
about the justice that lies everywhere in the world:
as in the spade I will use this evening
to turn under the row of peas whose leaves burn
with fire blight, brought on by frequent rain
and evening mist, and the disfigurement
we recognize as judgment in everything.

The Bird Feeders

Paradise organizes itself
around the double-trunked linden
that's pinned like a prayer wheel
with plastic bird feeders and suet nets,
and includes a child dressed
in bright pajamas like a goldfinch.
The child's father in a brown
terry-cloth robe lowers the feeders
to the ground, where he pours seed
straight from plastic bags, spilling it
over his bare feet.

The child points to the yellow pearls
and black, beak-shaped hulls
that bounce and ricochet
over the patio. And though
he knows the lazy pigeons
will walk their circles around
this overspill, he wants to show
his father the crazy motion
of the seed, how the seed comes alive
in his father's hands and dances
everywhere, disappearing in the coils
of the green hose and in the shade
of the green weeds. His father nods
and hoists the clear granaries
to their places, where they rock,
green and yellow roofed.

Beneath the shade of the linden,
father and son wait
as the downy woodpeckers thread
back along the trunk to the suet,
and the female cardinal, russet
in her shyness, waits for the red
finches and sparrows to leave.
In this back-yard paradise
the creatures are perfected
by delight. As if by feeding them
we provide for our own longing,
to lift off into the lightness
a child feels when he raises
his yellow arms to sight starlings
that drop like leaves into trees.

Night Waltz

Nights when we are further
than sleep, back somewhere
in the shadowy rooms of childhood,
deaf to any commotion, to
any complaint, the useless
and broken possessions of our lives
begin to stir. An old mattress
rolls out from the porch, a chair
descends from its ceiling hook
to walk unimpaired on wobbly legs,
or a couch rises on end. The doors
of apartments open and beyond
the earthly cycle of noise
the disheveled population tips
its way downstairs to dance
in the courtyard. In the moonless night
the things remember how hard
they were kept: how they were loyal
even to the edge of dreams;
working for little love,
and always the threat
of some weekend eviction, or worse,
a selling-off and carting-away
to poorer surroundings.
But they got free of neglect,
came out and met similar lives,
as if each apartment held a
sad memento of bondage,
or as if the will itself
were a badge of survival.

As morning nears,
these things lie down under the hood
of a dumpster or in the grass
along curbs, and we, back
from sleep, are surprised
by the litter, the abandonment,
as if the trashy ground
engendered mandibles of sofa beds,
refrigerators with unhinged doors,
the blue insides cool and inviting us
to imagine an ascension
into the next world, where suffering
is rewarded with glue, oil,
and electricity.

The Daughters of Degas

wake to the radio-alarm
in the next room. I know
how their plaid skirts lie
on white carpet, large white
blouses on the backs of blue
chairs. The dancers rise,
step into skirts, lift frail
hosiery from half-opened
drawers, white bras with
puckered seams. I know
how one stands on toes to
iron a shirt; another tilts
her head to unroll maroon
and pink curlers. But it
is grace or light or love
that smooths cloth or shapes
hair. That's what Degas
might say. Then suddenly
they hurry to gather books, pants
for p.e., tennis shoes,
pompons—everything cradled
between breasts and blue binders.
They blow me kisses off
their palms from the hallway
as they pass to the kitchen,
where Degas inspects them.
I enter their room, fall into
an unmade bed. The perfume
of an overture surrounds me,
and I think of my sisters

working quickly to fasten warm
buttons on their perfect blouses,
the air that made the cloth
billow as they tucked tails
into waistbands . . . my sisters
who taught me the revery
of this dance which I wake to
each morning in my own bed
and watch my wife rise
to fill the clothes around her,
or when, after she leaves,
I fall back to sleep,
then wake to see Degas
standing in the doorway,
calling out to me: *Son?*

White Bass

The white bass grew larger and larger
in the park lagoon, its milky shadow
enticing me to lower various baits
or to tie on lures named *Gray Darter* and *Miracle Marabou*.
The spiny fins winnowing water, gills as large as bear traps,
the white bass swam like an angel among lumbrous
carp and catfish: its beauty a kind of hope.

Years later, standing on the dock where aluminum canoes
lie like flatware in the sun, and looking over green water,
I hear a rod whip, and a shaggy line
arcs white and blue, plunking.
I drift and fall a little, wondering
if something large will strike me before I move,
before the reel clicks and I'm wound in, flashing and wobbling
on the leader, my flesh the flesh of the bass
or the flesh of my father, who lies, a few miles from here,
bare-chested with blue and white tubes entering and leaving him,
his body like an opaque aquarium, pumped and filtered.

Above him a screen wavers with schools of systole
and diastole. The green blips ascending like lantern fish
to a steady incandescence in which I hover, hiding a hook's
shank, and wait to be whipped over water, weighted,
suspended beneath the white side of a bobber
to see if my father swims by.

III

What Heals

When my niece brought her horse
from its winter stable into the sun
and led it over muddy earth, it ate bad straw
and sickened, then lay on the ground,
where its intestines were in danger of knotting.
She brought blankets
and waited through the night,
keeping the horse warm and still. Near dawn,
it regained its legs, and where the blankets
slipped from its back steam rose.
She rubbed the hard nose
and grabbed the fur behind its ears.

As I drove to the pasture that morning,
my sister told me that horses
were stupid because they saw things
four times larger than they were,
the road like a highway, mailboxes looming
like raised sheds, gaping snake holes,
or the monstrous car approaching the corral.
My niece turned calmly from her horse.
The huge blankets that had stilled the animal
draped the fence, and my niece's hands,
which had stroked its head all night,
darkened the sun as she waved.

Eyepiece

I had been thinking about the moon,
how you see it
from the back of a truck
at a neighbor's house—
emerald with a little gold—
while the neighbor reminds you not
to press too hard on the eyepiece.
I did once and the moon disappeared,
or something shut down
inside the telescope, and I was alone
on the truck, smaller than the tripod,
wondering how I'd lost
the big moon in the big sky.
Like once, home late from a party,
I stopped in the yard
to turn gray-white in moonlight.
The grass, a blue bristle,
blew back and forth unevenly,
and when I closed my eyes
a light filled my head.
Then my lover came outside and found me
lost in a privacy
that scared her. In bed
I told her I had been thinking
about the suicide of my college roommate.
Then I reassured her
and we tried to make love, but when
that part of ourselves that had shut down
so long ago began to open,
we pressed too hard

and were alone again. In a few weeks
I was too sullen to live with,
and like the moon
that disappeared from the eyepiece
at my neighbor's house
we couldn't be restored.
Those neighbors disappeared
from the block because of divorce:
how we all disappear under a moon
which my roommate said
hangs high in every neighborhood.

The Gazelles

They come now rising on spindly
sculpted legs, their heads nodding,
hooves dragging through weeds.
They rub their whiskery
chin tufts on the fence posts
near our feet, and when we reach
for the flat, white markings of their
foreheads, they won't be touched
but feign distraction in a browse
of nubbed grass, then raise
their heads again. What was it
they mistook in us? A detail
of eyelash from far away?
Our practiced look of wanting nothing?
And coming to us, as if
to freedom or a rare feeding, they
found we were like all humans
hoping to see themselves in friendly
beasts, using clucks and coos, ogling
for some response and, worse, what every
human tries eventually, a touch.
The need so great, we lean over fences
for the assurance the animals give.
But they compose themselves out of reach
and stare back over high grass and dark
boulders, continents and red earth.

The Jade Horse

Today, the dozen-stroke stone carving
transforms into the beast of my wish,
for the statue stands restlessly on my desk,
coaxing me onto its back,
where I bury my fists in its mane
and wait to rise out of my house,
to fly out over the familiar neighborhood.

But I rise no higher than my hand,
which holds the pale green horse to the window,
where I find white fissures branching
through its flesh, and though I want to prove
that death is only a monster,
only a goat filled with fire,
I return the horse to the desk,

where it becomes again an oddment
pawing among the unconnected treasures of coins
and shells, the circle of charms
that protects me from death's size
when it beckons me to ride
its small horse
or any beast of my wish.

Aquarium

The trigger fish and painted queens
add curves to their everlasting circuits
to avoid the woman working in the aquarium.

Blue scuba tanks striped with yellow
lightning bolts, red fins, orange gloves,
black skin, transform her into a species,

jury-rigged, though a patch of tan skin
between calf and thigh, like the cutaway
in a diagram, shows human tendon and muscle

flexing as she pedals, wipes the aquarium
glass with a cloth or dusts mottled armatures
of fake coral with a long boot brush.

Behind her mask her eyes are clear and dry,
but ringed with black mascara. Larger,
lighter, than our grounded selves who wave

to her, she waves to us, spits her mouthpiece
out, smiles, and pulls a glove off with her
teeth, then fits it to the air hose. The glove

fills and rises like a blowfish. Disturbed
to be seen by what we see, unconsciously
we hold our breath and wait until the woman

returns the mouthpiece to her mouth before
we exhale, letting go the bubbles of our wonder
and fear of the world behind glass, which we press

against to follow the woman's upward swim
as she retrieves the glove that bobs orange
and optically fat, a cloud in the aquarium's sky.

A Little Night Story

In back of El Minuto Café
beneath the tamarisk trees,
the ruined walls of an adobe church
protect the blue-and-red flicker
of votive candles. The tall clear
ones in the corner, stenciled
with irregular Guadalupes,
illuminate a plaque that tells
of a man whose wife ran away
with a priest. That was
a hundred years ago.

The man thought
if he sat under the trees
and cried, she'd return,
but whenever a woman passed,
he saw something of his wife's face.

One night, he was murdered
and dragged into the church.
The neighbors said the wind in the trees
was a sound like weeping,
and some have seen his face
calmed by these flames.

I zip up, walk back to the car.
As you drive home, I try to find
some infidelity in your face,
but there is only calmness.
I'm drunk. I'm slipping past you.
If I could weep,
you might never leave me.

Easter at San Xavier del Bac

This morning in the chapel
of the dead, a ceremony of color
rises in black smoke
behind a choir of photographs
torn from yearbooks, driver's
licenses, or cut from family
portraits. Each one, like
a leaf or insect held up
to light, floats transparent
behind votive candles
tiered in rows of blue
and red glass cups
that beat with their own light,
while the prayers of the living
hiss like flues
to keep the flames inspired,
urging the dead to rise
from the altar above puddles
of wax, food offerings
of *posole* and moldy bread.

But the dead seem glad
for this shadowy home,
happy to survive as glimmerings,
for they have their Christ
tacked to a wall:

a large photograph in which
a teen-ager leans against
his blue low-rider Ford,
his girl next to him,
his arms stretched over the roof,
and his feet crossed at the curb,
while a watch fob looping
to his knees glistens
like a rosary of teeth.

Flyer

The hard work of his flesh stretches
over tiny bones like brittle canvas
wrapped around a crop duster's ribbed

fuselage and wings. He lies at an angle
in the massive bed, a plane abandoned
and skewed on the edge of an island runway.

On the ground bright with crushed shells,
the pilot walks away, refusing
to look back. Now his eyes float in dark

sockets, shiny with overhead light,
like bolts half-covered with oil.
They are heavy with their old purpose

of threading long forms, reckoning
a night approach, or landing on a carrier's
heaving deck. The oil that seethes

from each rivet is ink from the brain.
He lands, skids wild through the years,
until now, folded up, gray, ready to be lowered

like a jet into the hold of a carrier.
But he is more delicate than this mothballed
shell or engine block that I fill with the

sentiment of flight. Like some well-behaved
Icarus, I've watched part of an ingenious
life from a safe altitude, never imagining

through that distance who my father was
without his fur-collared aviator's jacket
and colorful squadron patch that said

all about bravery, and not this frail hand,
his hard fingers that wrap around my fingers,
his eyes bulging and weatherproofed.

Wedding Story

On your wedding night, having fallen asleep,
I rose in a dream of ascension, comic
but sincere, over Virginia, where your house sits
at the edge of tilted farmland, berry lanes
and pastures where cows graze with rusted
cranes and drilling rigs.

I saw the wedding party gathered under yellow pine
and tulip trees, while a lengthy rope swing
dropped like a pendulum from a high branch
and carried children back and forth
in a blur of friendly light.

Below me, four gentiles holding the corners
of your *huppah* rose as wind lifted the canopy
over house and trees. The contraption twirled
and the gentiles revolved like gold angels
on a Christmas engine. Their brass poles

like slender trumpets, or like bucket riders
holding the simple reins of their copper buckets, rising
with their begged-for loads of coal, accepting
the attention of the wedding guests: some who
ran to the field and waltzed through the dry grass,

coaxing the gentiles to land, and others who stood
as if waving bon voyage, 1925, late summer,
no fear of icebergs, paper streamers raining colorfully
like lines from a madman's diary, ecstatic, full
of the thrill of journey. I saw the canopy

collapse, and the gentiles dropped into trees,
hung on limbs and held their slender trumpets
like tribal leaders shaking a fly whisk,
gesturing now for love and now for faith, blessing the guests,
the bride and groom, who all remember these figures

as angels or spirits who blessed the good parts
of their lives. So I floated over Virginia,
afraid of nothing, hovering on currents as warm
as my wife's breath, which brushed my back and arms
all night and powered the little engine of my dream.

Mescal

The label shows two Aztec warriors dressed
in bright vests, loincloths of yellow deerhide
and orange leggings sewn with green feathers
above bare feet. The warriors lean in a half-crouch
toward each other on one leg, arms positioned
like boxers, and one fist wrapped in red leather,
the other holding a painted gourd. As we drink,
their skin turns from rich amber to the blue opaqueness
of glass down to the level of their waists, leaving
them half-pale, while a gold clarity rises
in our heads. The warriors dance,
small circles inside the borders of the label,
punching each other now and then, blows
to the head and chest, and chanting to the gods
of peyote, mescaline, tequila, and the local deity,
Mescal de Basatette, for help that each might conquer
his twin before the ground beneath their feet
is drained. The warriors
stumble and spin, have trouble finding each other
in the gummy sweat of the label, their arms
held out like children's in blindman's-buff.
And no matter what the gods do to pit man
against man, occasionally the warriors fall
into each other's arms, brothers in the dizzy
swirl of a dance. And then
when the warriors lie in peeled strips

on the table, we, who have been fighting friendship
a drink at a time, approach the worm in the bottle,
and slide it on the last drops of liquor,
until it lies on the table, gray and mealy
like a piece of brain. We cut the worm in half
and offer each other a piece that is impossibly large
but dissolves on our tongues like something
that's waited years and years to be touched.

The Clasp

See, how in a meticulous calm
I close the jaws, fitting the teeth
of the clasp, and coil the pearls
on the dresser top like a serpent
lowered into sleep. If I unhinged
the mouth, the teeth would glimmer
in the mirror like pebbles caught
in a tide line, a necklace of chance
that would stretch miles over
bark and foam, skirting the washed-up
skeletons, the husks and rinds
that lie like a bowerbird's last
baubles of elegance and attraction.
Here is the spiny vertebrae I rattle
for humor, here the red bobber
of fidelity, and there the blue
sandal I hold out for love.
But I have only the tiny adder's head
clasp staring at me, whose coiled
body is a string of blue kelp, all
bladder and beads, and if I opened
the mouth of what I've lulled asleep,
the viper, on waking, might strike
what it first sees: me, its tail.
And to that mirror that returns
everything to salt and sand, I bring
the lethal sleep, remembering the serpent
came from pearls, safe in their shells in the sea.

About the Author

Michael Collier has lived in London and has traveled widely—
from Northern Africa to Siberia and Japan. He has worked as
a plumber, house painter, and activist, holds a B.A. from
Connecticut College (1976), an M.F.A. from the University
of Arizona (1979), and won a 'Discovery'/*The Nation* Award in
1981. He has been director of poetry at the Folger Shakespeare
Library, and teaches at Johns Hopkins University. He is as-
sistant professor of English at the University of Maryland. He
lives in Baltimore.

About the Book

The Clasp was composed in Garamond #3 by G&S Typesetters,
Inc. of Austin, Texas. It was printed on 60 lb. Warren's Old
Style and bound by Thomson-Shore, Inc. of Dexter, Michi-
gan. The book design is by Joyce Kachergis Book Design and
Production of Bynum, North Carolina.

Wesleyan University Press, 1986.